SANTA BARBARA

SANTA BARBARA

Photography by David Muench

Text by David Temple

SKYLINE PRESS

Produced by Boulton Publishing Services, Toronto
Designed by Fortunato Aglialoro

© 1984 Chicago Review Press
SKYLINE PRESS is an imprint of Chicago Review Press

ISBN 1-55652-046-8, previously ISBN 0-19-540614-1
Printed in Hong Kong by Everbest Printing Company, LTD.,
through Four Colour Imports, LTD.

INTRODUCTION

Every schoolchild knows that Santa Barbara is the place of the marriage of the mountains and the sea; poets must have been present at the wedding, songwriters can recapture the melodies. Barbareños are daily enjoying the delights of the wedding feast.

The mountains are the Santa Ynez Mountains. The sea is the Santa Barbara Channel. The mountains are sandstone reaching up to almost 4,000 feet. They have rugged grandeur as their wedding garment. The channel is twenty miles wide. It has as its outer wall, sheltering it from the broad Pacific, the Islands of Anacapa, Santa Cruz, San Miguel and Santa Rosa. The wedding day is any day, although sometimes the sea will kick up a storm and the palms and the pines will bow to the wind. Rarely, maybe once a year, there will be a breath of snow to deck the wedding-cake, and all the parents will rush all the little children to the top of the mountain range so that they can touch their first snow.

Geologists, songwriters and storytellers have celebrated this marriage of the mountains and the sea. Perhaps the people of Santa Barbara understand it best when they leave behind the pages and the scores. With a true sense of wonder and a little awe they know what it means to live between the kneeling mountains and the praying sea.

Santa Barbara lies nestled by its Islands where Juan Rodríguez Cabrillo came poking the noses of his two little ships northward in the fall of 1542. Portuguese by birth but sailing in the service of Spain, he had captained the *San Salvador* and the *Victoria* from Navidad, on the coast of Mexico, in search of the Northwest Passage. The first European discoverer of California, Cabrillo lies buried on the island where he died a few months later, the island that his sailors named after him but that Sebastián Vizcaíno was to christen 'San Miguel'. Vizcaíno came along the coast sixty years after Cabrillo, in search of a good harbor for the great galleons of Spain. In his cockey little ship, the *San Diego*, he put up here for the night of 3 December 1602, and called the place 'Santa Barbara'.

Santa Barbara has always lived by the sea. First were the Chumash Indians, who kept up a brisk and busy traffic among the Islands in their big, heavy, canoes, caulked with the local tar that appears to this day on the beaches.

One hundred and eighty years after Vizcaíno there came the seaborne supplies for the founding of the Presidio and the Mission, brought to Santa Barbara after lengthy probings along the coast. In the first half of the nineteenth century Yankee traders from New England anchored at Santa Barbara after swift runs around the Horn. The United States fleet filled the roadstead with ships in 1905.

The city still lives with the freshness of the sea in its nostrils, and with the rising and falling of the fog-horn in thick weather. The breakwater shelters pleasure-craft and the fishing fleet. Swimmers enjoy the beaches and the adventurous challenge themselves with water-sports. The water is here and the sand is here and Santa Barbara loves them. The oil-rigs are out in the Channel—and Santa Barbara endures them. Severe storms have swept away the sand, but nature has a way of bringing it back again. Quiet delight in the sea carries on, as does the fervor of the water-games.

Barbareños have a deep feeling for the Old Mission; they will tell you that it has always been there. There may be difficulties in proving that, for the town is in fact a little older than the Mission. Had it not been for a disagreement, the Presidio and the Mission would have set out together, but Governor Felipe de Neve stood on the high ground of his authority and the military settlement was established first in 1782. The Mission was founded four years later, in 1786. Even so, the Barbareño figures that he is pretty nearly right. The Mission was there when the first Chumash was laid to rest in the newly outlined 'God's Acre' in 1789. The Mission was not as large as it is now, it was not so stoutly built, but it was there. The Mission was there when Governor Pedro Fages wrote his report in 1787, and when the first roof-tiles were made in 1788. It had been there for some time when the Padre wrote to the Governor and asked that a rocket-maker be sent for the service of the Mission. The Mission was there in 1817 when Padre Ripoll wrote to the Governor of Alta California, Pablo Vicente de Solá—'Senor Gubernador, my companion tells me that you intimate to him that the herd of sheep which the Mission has in the Rancho del Refugio ought to be removed.' The Mission was doing well when the Indians for the first time participated in an election in 1822. Captain George Vancouver visited it on the crest of its hill in 1793 and Captain Duhaut-Cilly in 1822. The Mission carried on its work under the flags of Spain and Mexico and the United States. In Santa Barbara's mind the Old Mission is among the things that last forever.

Almost everyone remembers that Santa Barbara began with an argument. On Sunday morning 21 April 1782, everyone was set in his own direction. There were the Indians. There was the military. There was the church. Padre Junípero Serra was sure that he was founding a mission. Governor de Neve was certain that he was establishing only a presidio. Serra stood on good ground and stayed on it to the end. He wrote 'Mission' in the first register and he would not cross it out; but the Governor would not budge.

Barbareños who esteem both the fire of the Governor and the fervor of the Padre feel that both men erred in judgment. De Neve doubted that a mission would succeed. Perhaps he did not believe all that much in missions. Serra regarded the Presidio as poorly located. History proved them both wrong.

There was another party to the discussion. Yanunali, the Chumash chief, at first would not agree to starting anything at all. Later he relented.

Gradually the three strands were woven into one. The Indians helped build the Presidio. The fort later defended the Mission. The Chumash from the Mission manned the Presidio to repel the invader from the sea and so they protected both the town and the Mission.

There is on Santa Barbara the mark of Spain. There is a grace that stems from the days of the dons. By nature the place was sworn to beauty and by man it was pledged to graceful living, to refinement and to hospitality. The names and the descendants of the men and women who came out from Spain are everywhere,—the de la Guerras, the Carrillos, the Ortegas, the Cotas, the Covarrubias, the Orenas. Their names are on the streets. Their presence is felt in the councils of the city.

With the richness of Spanish culture there is also the toughness of purpose that marked the Spaniard. He put his fort and his chapel side by side. Because of the heritage of the firm purpose of Spain, the beauty of the arch remains and the strength of the tower and the coolness of the veranda and the music that still haunts hearts in the evening. In preserving its heirloom from Spain, Santa Barbara has shown it is tough, and does not intend to be swept off its feet by the tides of the times.

The gift of Spain is laid out before the visitor's eyes. He does not need a history book to tell him that Santa Barbara was founded by Spain. The Fiesta of the Old Spanish Days, which is held in August, brings back the full flood of the Spanish heritage as the whole town steps back 200 years and then dances forward into the present.

Water has always been the object of nervous search at Santa Barbara. With the abundance of Lake Cachuma the thirst of the people and of the land has been slaked but the Channel people are always nervous about their water supply.

In the Spanish beginnings the Presidio and, most of all, the Mission were resourceful in capturing the magic of water. In 1976 the American Society of Civil Engineers designated Santa Barbara Mission as a historic civil-engineering landmark and a salute was given to all civil engineers who were responsible for its conception, design, and construction.

The Presidio, soon after its founding, had begun to divert water from Pedregosa Creek. Fermín Francisco de Lasuén, Father-President of all the Alta California missions, had a vision of larger things as, with a sharp eye, he chose the site for the Mission in 1786. The water system which the Mission developed was a triumph of frontier engineering. The city of Santa Barbara is still using one of the original reservoirs for the local water system.

The Indian Dam, built in 1807 to impound the water from the mountains, even now remains intact. Still evident are the remains of a diversion dam constructed in Rattlesnake Canyon. Traces of the aqueducts which conducted the water can be found in many gardens. On the little hill above the Mission is the settling tank to desilt the water. Also there is the large upper reservoir to hold the supply, with gravity-flow to the mill to grind the grain, and then passage to the lower reservoir whence the water was conducted by stone aqueducts, still partly visible, to the orchard, the garden, the Moorish fountain, the Indian Village and the outdoor community laundry. Although the system is now about 170 years old, modern engineers still get excited about it and comment on the high quality of workmanship and the remarkable engineering skills demonstrated by those Mexican and Indian workmen long ago.

One of the brave days in Santa Barbara's history came in 1818, when Hippolyte de Bouchard, a French-born privateer, engaged in the service of independent Mexico and flying the flag of independent Buenos Aires, but ravaging the coast on his own account, appeared in the Channel. He had sacked the fort and town of Monterey in the week of 20–27 November and had enflamed the whole coast with fear as he moved southward. Women and children, with all the valuables that could be gathered, had been readied for removal to the interior. Sentinels were placed along the coast to spread news of the advance of the invader. Padre Luis Martinez, from the north, wrote to de la Guerra, as he sighted the menacing black-painted craft, 'If only I had two cannon, I could have the ships.' Padre Ripoll organized the Indians into companies; for this they chose their own sergeants and corporals. Indian archers made ready to man the Presidio with bows and arrows; for good measure they also carried their chopping knives.

Bouchard and his band landed at Refugio Beach, where they plundered the Ortega ranch and killed some cattle, but when the marauder appeared at Santa Barbara, it seems he was unready for combat with de la Guerra. Bouchard anchored in the Channel for several days then, measuring his chances, sent a flag of truce. He settled for an exchange of prisoners and then continued south to San Juan Capistrano, where he looted the Mission on 14–15 December. Meanwhile, however, there was great pride in Santa Barbara and a tide of joy at the Mission there, where the Indians had stood ready to fight a terrifying foe in order to save their home and the work of their hands.

With the tides of the times the Yankees appeared at Santa Barbara, coming in fast ships that cut around the Horn. They traded for hides and tallow. There were some of these New Englanders who settled down and married the fair ladies of the new land. Spanish names became interwoven with Chapmans and Thompsons and Hills. The men who had come on the swift ships offered special services in town or settled on ranches which came to know the Danas and the Elwells and the Foxens. The Yankee set his roots here and left his mark. Santa Barbara would never become New England, but there would be some gables that would speak of Massachusetts and some fences that would recall Maine. There was something of the Yankee that stayed.

A Barbareño could not live without his gardens. Since the first planting days of the Spaniards, gardens have been a support and a delight. The native American along the Channel was not a planter but a seed-gatherer. The birds had planted and the winds had sown the seed, but it was not until 29 April 1783 that the Presidio in Santa Barbara planted the first wheat. In the late summer there was a small harvest. The cycle had begun. De la Guerra would plant a garden. The Mission would develop great fields of wheat. Ortega would plant corn.

The gardens of the townhouses were mostly geometric in the Spanish tradition. They had grapevines, artichokes and, interspersed with the green garden growth, hollyhocks and the Rose of Castile. The Mission had great gardens, an orchard, and two vineyards with 3695 stocks.

The gardeners of Santa Barbara are busy still, as they gather trees and shrubs from all round the world. These imports generally thrive because of the benign and temperate climate. Trees from many countries line the streets and enhance the favored plots of homes where we find the Spanish fir, the silver wattle from Australia, the witch-hazel from Iran, the mastic tree from Kashmir and the wine palm from Chile.

The story of Santa Barbara is told in the names of its streets. These recall Yanunali and Anapamu the Chumash chief, and Valerio the Indian outlaw and Anacapa the island which, so the Indians said, appeared and disappeared like a will-of-the-wisp. Cabrillo commemorates the great explorer. Three streets recall the famous 'lost cannon'. Because the artillery had disappeared, Colonel Mason levied a fine of 500 pesos against the town. The Barbareños perpetuated the memory of the incident in the street names of Canon Perdido, Mason, and Quinientos. The names of great families are on the streets—de la Guerra, Carillo, Ortega, Cota and Gutierrez. Similarly a long passage of history is evoked by the names of Spanish and Mexican governors—Figueroa, Solá, Arrellaga and Micheltorena. Salsipuedes, or 'Get-Out-If-You-Can', was a rough street and Punta Gorda, the 'fat point' was at one time an important artery. Castillo used to have a little fort looking out toward the sea, and Islay recalls the wild cherry which drew the Indians to the mountains as spring turned into summer.

Chumash Indians, Franciscan missionaries, Spanish soldiery, Yankee sailors, French privateers, pioneer ranchers and in later times artists and writers of renown, all played their parts in the long and vivid history of Santa Barbara. The glory of its setting, the colors of its flowers, the grace of the

Mission and the vigorous character of its tree-girt streets combine to make of Santa Barbara one of the loveliest places in America. Some of its beauty is depicted in this book.

FATHER DAVID TEMPLE, OFM
Old Mission, Santa Barbara, California, 1983

1 Old Mission, Santa Barbara

Santa Barbara Mission was founded in 1786 for the Chumash Indians of the Santa
Barbara Channel. It was the tenth in the chain of Missions pioneered by Padre
Junípero Serra. It is the only Mission to continue without interruption under the care
of the founding Franciscans throughout its two hundred years of history..

2 Cold Springs Canyon, Montecito

This little fall tumbles in a tiny splendor of water on the eastern fork of Cold Spring Creek in Montecito, which adjoins Santa Barbara. The water is very cold, in contrast to nearby Hot Springs Creek where the springs are so hot that they attracted the Indians and later American visitors. The old Montecito mansions often had, among several water systems, one of water from the Hot Springs.

3 *(right)* Old Mission, Santa Barbara

The Mission church (1815–20) was built of native sandstone by the Chumash Indians, according to the plan of the Franciscan Mission Padres. The site was previously occupied by three successive adobe churches. In designing the church, Padre Antonio Ripoll drew freely from Vitruvius' *De Architectura*, written in the time of Caesar Augustus. In a master stroke Ripoll added to the original Greco-Roman design two additional columns for the facade and also two massive Spanish towers. The church, which also includes Moorish elements, represents 2000 years of architectural tradition. Visitors have always been amazed at the boldness of the plan and the perseverance of the execution.

4 *(left) Agave attenuata*, Covarrubias Adobe, Santa Barbara

This eye-catching, drought-resistant plant is native to Mexico. When, after some twelve years, it blooms, it sends out a long curving stalk like the trunk of an elephant.

5 Courtyard and Bell Tower, Old Mission, Santa Barbara

Over the Mission's famous Sacred Garden looms the majesty of the west tower and the ancient bells. Some of these bells were cast by Manuel Vargas in Peru and by Manuel Ruelas in Mexico. Some of the Mission bells were three years old when George Washington took the oath of office. In the original arrangement, three bells hung on one yoke for ringing and three bells were mounted in a stationary position for tolling.

6 *(left)* Covarrubias Adobe, Santa Barbara

This early adobe was built in 1817 by Domingo Antonio Ignacio Carrillo. With its long *sala* of over 50 feet it was for many decades the center of social life in Santa Barbara. The Mission Indians built the thick adobe walls, made the roof tiles and mounted them on willow cane set on adobe. The Carrillos married into the most important families of California: the de la Guerras, the Sepulvedas, the Picos, the Yorbas and others. The Carrillo-Covarrubias family occupied this house for almost a full century. On many occasions California's official government business was conducted from this adobe.

7 Moreton Bay Fig

The Moreton Bay Fig, *Ficus macrophylla*, native to Australia, was planted in the Old Mission cemetery about 1890. It has a crown spread of 93 feet and a trunk circumference of 22 feet.

8 *(left) Pueblo Viejo*, Santa Barbara

On 21 April 1786 Governor de Neve founded the Presidio. Padre Junípero Serra said the mass, raised the cross and sang the 'Alabado'. This was the fourth of the royal Presidios or forts established by Spain to hold the land and to repel intruders. The Santa Barbara Presidio became the headquarters of the second military district. Many changes and successive developments have altered the original Presidio area as laid out by de Neve and as executed by José Francisco Ortega, the first *commandante*. At the present time remarkable progress has been made in restoring the original Presidio compound.

9 Valley oak, *Quercus lobata*

The Spaniards, in the first days of exploration, found this great native oak widely dispersed. They cut crosses in these oak trees to mark the original 'Camino Real', the 'King's Highway'.

10 Exhibit of candle-making, previously at the Old Mission, Santa Barbara

Candle-making was one of the early crafts. At the Old Mission the Indians were instructed in the process of dipping and then drying the candles. They learnt how to use the candles in lanterns and holders with reflectors and mirrors in order to increase their light.

11 *(right)* Ruins of outlying building, Old Mission, Santa Barbara

At the Old Mission the Chumash Indians became competent craftsmen. For the Indian Village on the Mission grounds they constructed for themselves 252 adobe houses with tile roofs. At the Mission there were shops and buildings adjoining the main complex, where the native men became skilled in woodworking, blacksmithing, tanning and many other trades, while their wives and daughters were instructed in sewing and dress-making.

12 *(left)* Flamingoes, Child's Estate, Santa Barbara Zoo
The Child's Estate comprises 16 acres. It is now a city park and zoo and is maintained for cultural and recreational purposes. This wooded property was the site of an Indian village or *ranchería*.

13 Moorish fountain (1808), Old Mission, Santa Barbara
While the Chumash Indians were schooled in work habits at the Mission, there was also time for excursions, holidays, hunting and fishing. Often the work assigned could be finished by noon. For the rest of the day the Indians were free and could divert themselves with music, dancing and games.

14 *(left)* Sunken Garden and County Courthouse, Santa Barbara

The Santa Barbara County Courthouse was built from 1926 to 1929. It recalls Santa Barbara's Hispanic heritage. In brilliant lines it follows the styles of Spanish, Moorish and Mediterranean architecture. The Sunken Garden with its raised steps provides a platform for 'Fiesta' dances in the first full moon of August. It also offers an ideal setting for county and city functions.

15 El Paseo, Santa Barbara

El Paseo is like a bit of Old Spain. It has been beautifully developed about the de la Guerra adobe where José Antonio, the *Gran Capitán*, himself from Old Spain, built with the aid of Indian labor a fair house which is still the pride of the city. El Paseo now takes off from this with attractive shops and with a world-famous restaurant on the spot of the *potrero* or horse corral of the original holding.

EL MARQUÉS DE VIANA Y DEL VALLE DE LA PALOMA, CONDE DE URBASA, CABALLERIZO, BALLESTERO Y MONTERO MAYOR DE SU MAJESTAD CATÓLICA DON ALFONSO XIII REY DE ESPAÑA, VISITÓ ESTA CIUDAD DE Sta BÁRBARA EL DIA 4 DE OCTUBRE DE 1924. Y EN RECUERDO DE ESTA FECHA DONÓ ESTA INSCRIPCIÓN A DON BERNARDO HOFFMANN DIGNO PROPAGANDISTA DE LA ARQUITECTURA ANDALUZA Y DE LOS HISTÓRICOS RECUERDOS

16 Commemorative Plaque, El Paseo,
    Santa Barbara

The plaque recalls that the Marquis of Viana and of Valle de la Paloma, Count of Urbasa, bearer of honors from King Alfonso XIII of Spain, visited Santa Barbara on 4 October 1924, and that in memory of this date he set up this inscription to honor Bernard Hoffmann who had done so much to foster an appreciation of Andalusian architecture and of the memories of Spain.

17 *(right)* Assembly Room of Board of Supervisors, County Courthouse, Santa Barbara

The supervisors sit at the semi-circular carved desk. The murals were done by Dan Sayre Groesbeck. They depict in dramatic fashion the history of Santa Barbara.

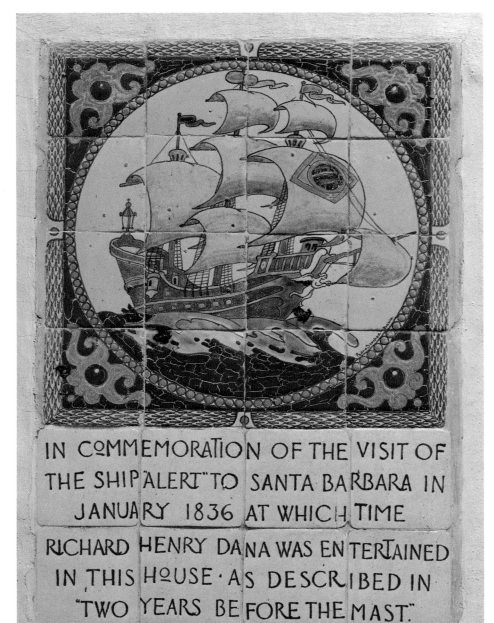

IN COMMEMORATION OF THE VISIT OF
THE SHIP "ALERT" TO SANTA BARBARA IN
JANUARY 1836 AT WHICH TIME
RICHARD HENRY DANA WAS ENTERTAINED
IN THIS HOUSE · AS DESCRIBED IN
"TWO YEARS BEFORE THE MAST."

18 Commemorative Plaque, Santa Barbara

19 County Courthouse, Santa Barbara

This plaque in the Great Anacapa Arch commemorates the completion of the courthouse in which the hallways are rendered in *mudejar* and stencilled patterns of ancient Moorish origin.

20 Main tower detail, County Courthouse, Santa Barbara

The courthouse was planned to house all county government. The architect was William Mooser of San Francisco, who was aided by his son who had just returned after seventeen years in Spain.

21 (right) *Cymbidium*

Orchids thrive in Santa Barbara. The *cymbidium*, which is perhaps the most popular group of the orchid family, is cultivated by many private and professional growers and appears in splendor at the Santa Barbara International Orchid Show, which attracts exhibits from many nations. In the 1983 show one hundred judges granted awards for exhibits by many growers from far and near.

DIOS · NOS · DIO · LOS · CAMPOS
EL · ARTE · HVMANA · EDIFICO · CIVDADES

22 *(left)* El Quartel Adobe, Santa Barbara

'El Quartel', or 'the soldier's quarters', is the oldest building retaining its original integrity in Santa Barbara. It was built about 1788 and formed part of the family housing in the west wing of the Presidio quadrangle. Originally a soldier's family used the backyard for cooking, laundering and keeping domestic animals.

23 Archway, County Courthouse, Santa Barbara

This Great Anacapa Arch is made of locally quarried sandstone. The inscription proclaims that God gave us the country and that the skill of man has built the town. The medallions of Industry and of Agriculture are sculptured in local sandstone by Ettore Cadorin. Queen Elizabeth II of England passed through this archway for the official County and City ceremonies in March 1983.

24 Bell Tower, La Purísima Mission

La Purísima Concepción Mission, founded in 1787, has been restored to its original condition by the Civilian Conservation Corps in concert with the State of California. The restored Mission now stands as an exact reproduction of the original, down to some of the smallest details.

25 *(right)* Shoreline bluffs, Goleta Beach

A century ago Alexander Peter More mined asphalt along this coastline that was used for paving the streets of San Francisco. He also landed sheep here from his Santa Rosa Island rancho. The Santa Barbara campus of the University of California has been located here since 1954.

26 Courtyard and Tower, near El Presidio, Santa Barbara

The Presidio was founded by order of King Carlos III of Spain in order 'to provide benefits of government for the inhabitants of the Santa Barbara Channel area'. The first *Commandante* was Lt José Francisco Ortega. He was followed by José Raimundo Carrillo and by José Antonio de la Guerra.

27 Courtyard fountain, Santa Barbara Historical Society

The Santa Barbara Historical Society building is located on the edge of the historic
city of Santa Barbara. It literally 'sprang from the soil', being made of 70,000 adobe
bricks fashioned from the soil of the spot. The 16,000 roof tiles and 12,000 floor tiles
were handmade in several Mexican villages.

28 Museum of Natural History, Santa Barbara

The Santa Barbara Museum of Natural History is located on eleven acres in the Mission Canyon. Having started with a collection of birds' eggs, the scope of the Museum holdings was later broadened to include all of natural history. The Museum provides exhibits and educational programs, with a focus on the Pacific southwestern United States and special emphasis on southern and coastal California.

29 *(right)* El Quartel Adobe, El Presidio, Santa Barbara

In the early 1800s a new gate was opened in the defense wall at the Presidio. The soldier living at El Quartel served as the guard. José Valenzuela was the gatekeeper in the late Mexican period and in reward for his services was given the deeds of the house in 1846.

30 *(left)* Stow House, Goleta

In 1872 the widow of Daniel Hill sold to William Whitney Stow 1043 acres of the easterly portion of Dos Pueblos Rancho. Stow placed his son Sherman in charge, and shipped lumber from San Francisco the following year. To avoid wharfage, the lumber was floated through the breakers onshore at Goleta. In 1875 Stow shipped and planted 3000 walnut trees and 9700 almond trees, followed by 3000 lemon trees. In turn Sherman's son, Edgar, took over the management in 1915, becoming a successful rancher, State Assemblyman and State Senator. In 1967 the family gave the Stow House to the County of Santa Barbara.

31 Palms, Alameda Park

Santa Barbara has an unparalleled display of palm trees. Botanists are fascinated by their number and variety. Among the most decorative are the Mexican Fan Palms, flanking the beach at Cabrillo Boulevard, and the Canary Island Date Palms, on both sides of Las Palmas Drive through Hope Ranch.

32 *(left)* Main entrance, Brooks Institute of
 Photography, Santa Barbara

'Grayholm' was the Montecito estate of David
Gray of Detroit. The mansion on Eucalyptus Hill
was snuggled among huge boulders. The stone-
masons fitted the stones by trimming them from
behind so that they left the lichen and sea-creature
fossils to view. The modest entranceway led into a
twenty-three room residence. Grayholm today is
the headquarters of the Brooks Institute of Photography, which has two additional campuses in
the Santa Barbara area.

33 Reservoir wall, Old Mission, Santa Barbara

Visitors to the Old Mission in the early 1800s were
intrigued by the water supply system as a feat of
engineering. Duhaut-Cilly marveled at a water
mill which Padre Ripoll was constructing, into
which water fell at an angle of about 35 degrees,
instead of vertically, with the wheel and its buck-
ets in a horizontal position.

34 Bottlebrush tree *(Callistemon citrinus)*, native to Australia

35 Yucca and bougainvillea,
County Courthouse, Santa Barbara

36 Lake Cachuma

Lake Cachuma is a man-made lake created by damming the Santa Ynez River. It is officially described as 'the Cachuma unit of the Santa Barbara County Water Project of the United States Bureau of Reclamation'. Tecolote Tunnel, which carries the Cachuma water through the Santa Ynez range, was five years under construction because of special difficulties. To the east and under snow are Mt McKinley and San Rafael Mountain, both over 6000 feet.

37 *(right)* Seminary

Young men who wished to follow the life of the Franciscan Padres were trained at the Old Mission. In 1899 the program was transferred to St Anthony's Seminary adjoining the Mission.

38 Spring wildflowers, foothills of
   San Rafael Mountains

Wildflowers appear in a great burst of color in the
spring. There are carpets of annuals (California
poppy, lupine, owl's clover) and generous blooms
from the shrubs (*ceanothus*, wild fuchsia and
monkeyflower).

39 West Beach, Santa Barbara

40 Lichen and valley oaks, Santa Barbara

41 *(right)* Sunrise, Goleta Beach

Since *goleta* means 'schooner' in Spanish, the
name of the town may derive from some modest
shipbuilding. In 1828 Carlos Antonio Carrillo and
William Goodwin Dana had a schooner built for
coastal trading and otter hunting. Or the name
may commemorate an American schooner long
ago stranded in the estuary.

From the earliest days the Goleta Indian villages were the most populous of all. Portolá esti-
mated the inhabitants at 1500. Santa Barbara
Mission worked the fertile fields and created its
San José vineyard here.

42 Nasturtium and live oak, *(Quercus agrifolia)*

The Santa Barbara oaks were found to be too contorted to be used in building operations and the lack of suitable timber of sufficient size was a great problem in early Santa Barbara construction. De la Guerra brought the pine timbers for his house by ship from Monterey. The Mission may have transported the roof beams for the church from the Santa Barbara Islands; when the Indians built their own houses in the Mission Village, they supplied the timber from locations known to them in the mountains.

43 Cattle and oaks, Santa Ynez Valley

The Santa Ynez Valley provided large pasturelands for the cattle of the Santa Barbara Mission, which established ranches there, stocking them also with sheep, goats and horses. The best of the arable land was sown with wheat, corn, barley, beans and peas. When the Mission Santa Ynez was founded in 1804, 112 of the neophytes from Santa Barbara moved to Santa Ynez.

44 *(left)* San Rafael Wilderness and Sierra Madre Mountains

The San Rafael Mountains form the eastern rampart of the Santa Ynez Valley. They rise above 6500 feet. Pioneers were drawn to these rugged slopes by the hunting. Quicksilver mining later came on apace.

There are tales of the 'mountain men' who scoured the San Rafaels. One such unforgettable character was Davy Brown. Born in Ireland, he trapped in the West with Kit Carson. In the Southwest he fought in the Texas-Mexican War and joined the Texas Rangers. In 1879 he appeared in the back-country of Santa Barbara, where he was raising horses and mules near Zaca. He is reported to have lived in a hollow sycamore log in 1883. Later he built a cabin in Fir Canyon, where he reckoned as his own mountain reserve all the rugged slopes within a radius of twenty-five miles.

45 Pastures in Santa Ynez Valley

In the 1930s the Valley was known as the Valley of the Palomino, because of the success of Dwight Murphy in developing this strain of horse at Rancho Los Prietos. Cattle-raising was general, but in the 1970s this gave way in large part to horse ranches, with a great preference for exclusively Arabian breeds.

46 Forest cascade above Montecito, Santa Ynez Range

47 *(right)* Live oak grove and creek, Santa Ynez Valley

The California live oak, *Quercus agrifolia*, grows freely in the foothills and valleys and has been introduced as a decorative shade-tree in gardens. It grows to a height of seventy feet, with strong, thick limbs, and trunks that are several feet across.

48 *(left)* Solvang

In 1910 a committee of Danish-Americans in Michigan decided to found a Danish colony in California and bought 9000 acres of the Rancho San Carlos de Jonata in the Santa Ynez Valley. They were intent upon forming a folk school as well as a Danish settlement. In 1914 they opened Atterdag College, which later became a cultural center.

49 Solvang

Skilled artisans came to Solvang, bringing the touch of Denmark to the town. Danish architecture, customs, foods and festivals are highlighted. In 1939 the Crown Prince Frederick of Denmark and Princess Ingrid visited the colony and later returned several times.

50 Poppyfield, Little Pine Mountain

Little Pine Mountain and Big Pine Mountain in the San Rafael Range rise to a height of 6828 feet.

51 *(right)* Mission Santa Ynez

This was the nineteenth of the California Missions. It was founded in 1804 in the ample valley and amid the populous *rancherías* of Indians 48 miles north of Santa Barbara. Well preserved is the original Indian mural work in the decoration of the interior of the church. The use of the Greek key in the adornment of the sacristy walls is intriguing.

52 University of California Santa Barbara shoreline, Goleta

In the foreground are Fish Rocks from which Indians and other anglers have fished for centuries. The Regents of the University of California were awarded the former military training base at Goleta in 1948. The University of California Santa Barbara opened at this location in 1954.

53 *(right)* Monterey Cypress, Santa Barbara coast

The Monterey Cypress, *Cupressus macrocarpa*, thrives in Santa Barbara. In the distance is Rincon Hill.

54 *(left)* Lake los Carneros, Santa Ynez Park

'Los Carneros', or 'the rams', is believed to be
named from a natural topographical phenomenon
in the source of the mountain stream. The present
Carneros Lake was developed by Edgar Stow
from a reservoir that in turn had been developed
from little more than a pond.

55 Nojoqui Falls

The Indians called the place 'Naxuwi' which the
Spanish wrote 'Najue' or 'Anajue'. The meaning is
unclear, although some say it means 'honeymoon'
and others say 'night hawk', perhaps in deference
to one or another of the numerous local legends.

56 Santa Barbara from the Mesa

The Mesa or tableland was chosen in 1865 by the
United States Government for the placement of a
thirty-foot lighthouse. This was electrified in 1921
but destroyed by the earthquake of 1925. It was
replaced by the present automated lighthouse on
the same site.

57 Valley oak, Santa Ynez Valley

The temperate climate, the good hunting and the abundance of acorns from the oak trees attracted the Chumash to the Santa Ynez Valley about the year AD 1000. The Indians also took steelhead trout from the year-round river.

58 *(left)* Yacht harbor, Santa Barbara

Santa Barbara was for decades a seaport without an adequate harbor. In the early 1800s trading vessels anchored a mile and a half off shore. To assist ships in unloading cargo a rather short wharf was built in 1865 and a much longer one in 1872.

59 Grasses, La Cumbre Park,
   Los Padres National Forest, Santa Ynez Range

Los Padres is one of the seventeen National Forests of California. It lies within Santa Barbara Ventura, San Luis Obispo and Kern Counties.

60 Arroyo Burro Beach Park

The bluffs above Arroyo Burro Beach offer a fine vantage point for whale watching during the season of migration.

61 *(right)* Yacht harbor, Santa Barbara

The sponsor of the yacht harbor was Major Max Fleischmann, who supported many public projects. In order to provide a harbor of quality for his yacht the *Haida*, Max Fleischmann, who left a legacy of generosity in his care for the city and the Mission, spent over $600,000 in the 1920s for the building of the breakwater which shelters private craft and the fishing fleet.

62 *(left)* Andrée Clark Bird Refuge

In the east part of the City of Santa Barbara, which ran into lagoons and marshes, the Andrée Clark Bird Refuge now offers a freshwater lake for resident and migratory birds. This was effected principally by the donation of Huguette Clark in memory of her daughter, Andrée Clark.

63 Santa Barbara Channel from Santa Ynez Range

Richard Henry Dana described Santa Barbara's waterfront as he saw it in *Two Years Before the Mast*: 'The bay, or as it is commonly called, the Canal of Santa Barbara, is very large, being formed by the mainland on one side....which here bends like a crescent, and three large islands opposite to it and at the distance of twenty miles.'

64 Live oaks, Santa Ynez Valley

65 *(right)* Blue *Ceanothus*

The *Ceanothus*, or California lilac, in a number of varieties, and varying in blossoms from white to deep blue, is present in abundance on the sunny slopes.

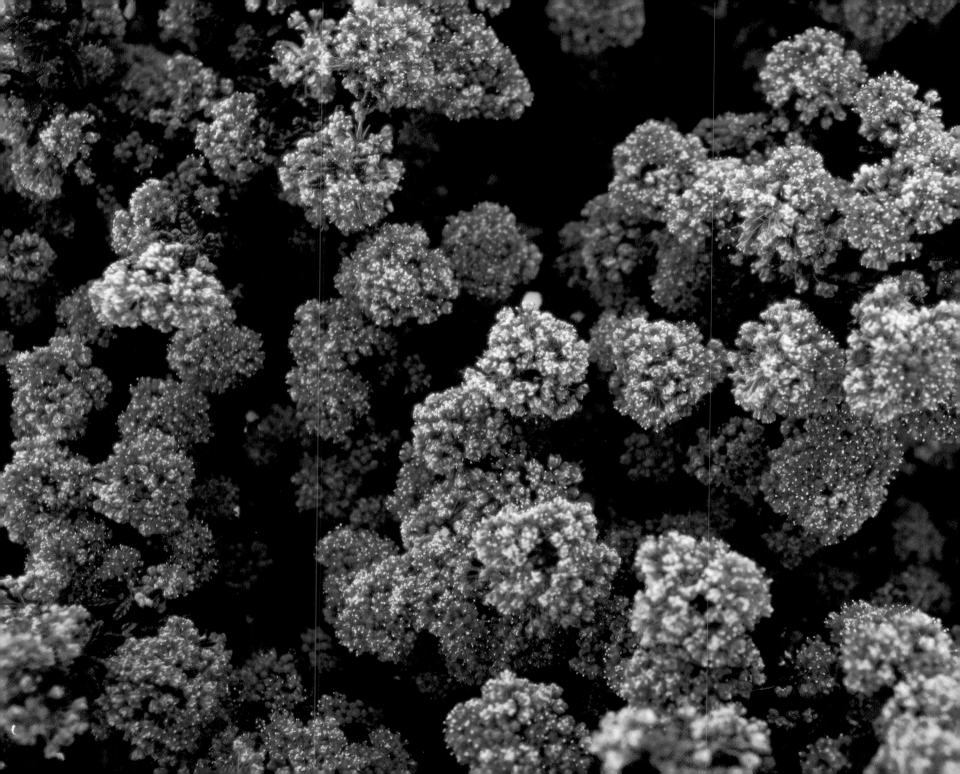

66 *Cattleya*

67 *(right)* Tidal pool at sunset

68 *(left)* Sunrise, East Beach, Santa Barbara

69 Coast range above Jalama

Jalama was the 'xalam', meaning 'bundle', of the Chumash who had a village along the creek.

70 Mission Creek, Santa Barbara Botanic Garden
The Garden was established to study native California plants in appropriate settings. It also concentrates on native plants in order to determine their uses in present-day gardens. The Old Mission Dam, which was built of native sandstone by the Indians under the direction of the Franciscan Padres, is within the Garden properties.

71 Santa Barbara Rose Garden

The City Rose Garden is in the Mission Historical Park, which preserves the
Mission's old waterworks, ruins of sandstone-wall shops and the tannery vats. The
Garden shares the Mission's California Landmark status. The garden is one of
twenty test-gardens in the United States for All-American Rose Selection.

72 Work-out at Hope Ranch

Hope Ranch, located at the southeastern end of the Goleta Valley, is a distinguished
residential park. It was once the Mexican land grant called Las Positas Rancho,
which later became the Thomas Hope Ranch.

73 Oaks and sage, foothills of Figueroa Mountain

Figueroa Mountain in the San Rafael Range has an altitude of 4528 feet. It is named for José Figueroa who was governor of California from 1833 to 1835. He is buried in the crypt beneath the sanctuary of the church of Santa Barbara Mission.

74 Los Padres National Forest, Coast Range

75 *(right)* Valley oaks

76 *(left)* Santa Ynez Range

77 Sand dunes at Oso Flaco Lake

Of great interest are the sand dunes at Oso Flaco or 'lean bear', and the Rancho
Guadalupe Dunes. Cecil B. de Mille filmed *King of Kings* at this latter site in the
1920s.

78 Evening, Jalama Beach

79 *(right)* Spring, south side of Santa Ynez Range
Arlington Peak is in the background. The *Ceanothus crossifolius*, or 'Snowball', is
common above 3000 feet along the summits of the Santa Ynez Mountains, where
it is found mostly on south slopes.

80 *(left)* Natural bridge, Goleta Beach

Near this natural bridge there was, in the high days of the trade, a whaling station with huge rendering pots. The bridge was formed by wave action undermining the cliff, but was washed out during the 'El Niño' storms of the 1982–83 season.

81 Santa Barbara, with Arlington and Granada Buildings

82 Santa Barbara Rose Garden

The City Rose Garden is one of 130 accredited rose gardens in the nation. It regularly reports some 900 plants with 80 or more varieties. Neighbors and volunteers groom and prune the bushes to assure continued accreditation. The Little Gardens Club installed a fragrance garden for the blind in 1971.

83 *(right)* Dawn along the Santa Barbara coastline

84 Pacific sunrise with palms, Santa Barbara coast

85 *(right)* Old Mission, Santa Barbara, at dusk

Santa Barbara is known as 'the Queen of the Missions'. There are many who have contributed to her majesty. There was the greatness of the dream of the Spaniard. This in large part came true because of the advancing skill of the Indian. There was the daring of Padre Ripoll, who was not afraid to try too much and who feared rather that he would do too little. There is the pride of the city, which has always been solicitous for the throne of its queen. There has been the generosity of friends and benefactors, who have cared for the towers on the hillside and after the earthquakes have brought back their splendor.

86 Sunset over eucalyptus-covered headlands, from Ortega Hill, Santa Barbara